NATIONAL
GEOGRAPHIC
KiDS

MYTHS

BUSTED!
2

JUST WHEN YOU
THOUGHT YOU KNEW
WHAT YOU KNEW . . .

By Emily Krieger
Illustrations by Tom Nick Cocotos

NATIONAL GEOGRAPHIC
WASHINGTON, D.C.

Tomato
Juice

CONTENTS

MYTH

THERE'S NO GRAVITY IN SPACE.

ORIGIN
People often talk about experiencing weightlessness in space because of zero gravity.

BUSTED!

GRAVITY IS THE FORCE OF ATTRACTION BETWEEN ANY TWO OBJECTS WITH STUFF.

You're made of stuff. So is Earth. Earth has way more stuff than you, though. So its force of attraction, or pull, on you is much stronger than your pull on it. That's what keeps your feet on the ground. In turn, the sun's greater gravity, extending throughout our solar system, is what keeps Earth and the other planets orbiting the star. So there's gravity everywhere, even in space. The term "zero gravity" does not actually mean an absence of gravity. In fact, Earth's gravity, which extends into the space around it, is what keeps astronauts in orbit around the planet.

The International Space Station and everything aboard it—including the astronauts—orbit Earth at a SPEED OF 17,500 MILES AN HOUR (28,000 KM/H)!

TOMATOES
ARE
VEGETABLES.

ORIGIN

Botanists, or scientists who study plants, consider the tomato a fruit. Despite this, in 1893 the U.S. Supreme Court ruled that the tomato is a vegetable.

BUSTED!

SCIENTIFICALLY SPEAKING, A FRUIT CONTAINS SEEDS AND DEVELOPS FROM THE OVARY OF A PLANT. A vegetable is another edible part of the plant, such as the leaves (cabbage) or root (carrots). The Supreme Court judges ruled that tomatoes are vegetables because of the way we eat them, "usually served at dinner in, with, or after the soup, fish, or meats . . . and not, like fruits generally, as dessert."

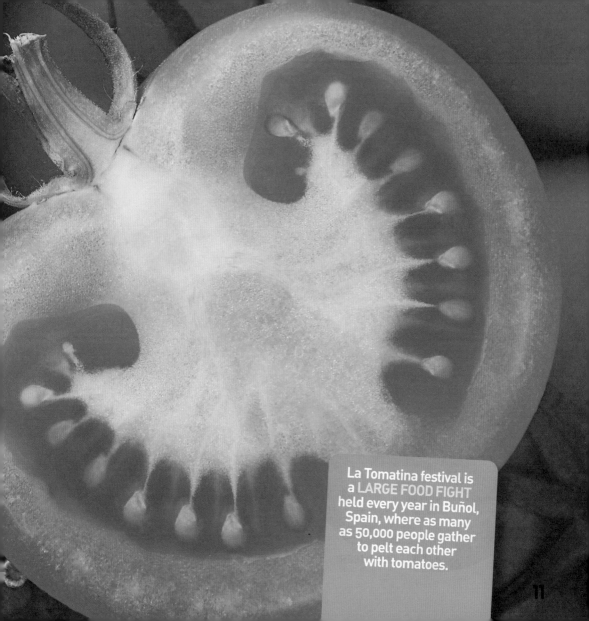

La Tomatina festival is a **LARGE FOOD FIGHT** held every year in Buñol, Spain, where as many as 50,000 people gather to pelt each other with tomatoes.

11

OTHER "VEGETABLES" THAT ARE ACTUALLY FRUITS

AVOCADO

CUCUMBER

PEPPERS

SQUASHES

ZUCCHINI

EGGPLANT

GREEN BEANS

13

MYTH

YOU SHOULD POOP AT LEAST ONCE A DAY.

ORIGIN

It's unknown where exactly this idea comes from. But "staying regular," or pooping frequently enough, is important. The process removes waste from the body that would otherwise build up and cause harm.

NOVEMBER

Monday	Tuesday	Wednesday	Thursday	Friday	Saturday	Sunday
27	28	29	30	31	~~1~~	~~2~~
~~3~~	~~4~~	~~5~~	6	7	8	9
10	11	12	13	14	15	16
17	18	19	20	21	22	23
24	25	26	27	28	29	30

BUSTED!

A PERSON IS CONSIDERED CONSTIPATED WHEN THEY HAVE FEWER THAN THREE BOWEL MOVEMENTS PER WEEK. So, by definition, there's nothing wrong with you if you aren't pooping once a day, as long as you are pooping at least three times a week. How long it takes to "pass" food depends on a person's body and what they eat. It can take anywhere from less than a day to three days for food to make its grand exit.

Scientists estimate that the 81.5-ton (74-metric ton) *ARGENTINOSAURUS HUINCULENSIS* produced 3.9 gallons (15 l) of dino poop at a time!

OIL COMES FROM DEAD DINOSAURS.

ORIGIN

Oil, coal, and natural gas are all types of fossil fuels. These energy sources formed from the remains, or fossils, of organisms that lived hundreds of millions of years ago. Dinosaurs roamed Earth from about 230 million years ago to 65 million years ago, so a lot of oil must be made from them, right?

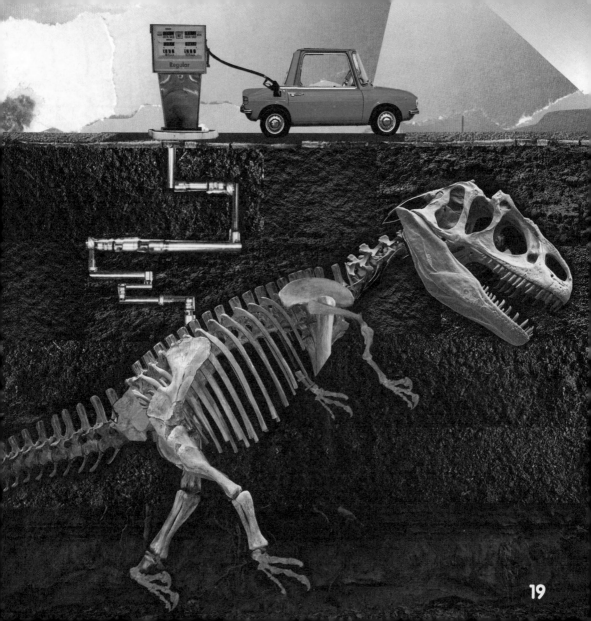

BUSTED!

OIL IS OLD. REALLY OLD.
The vast majority of it is made from tiny plants, animals, and bacteria that lived millions of years before the first dinosaurs existed!

COAL IS MADE FROM
PLANT—NOT ANIMAL—
remains. It takes ten feet
(3 m) of ancient plant
remains to make one foot
(0.3 m) of coal.

21

MYTH

IF YOU GO OUTSIDE WITH WET HAIR, YOU'LL CATCH A COLD.

ORIGIN

This myth has been passed down from generation to generation, though no one knows exactly where it began. It hinges on the idea that being cold causes a cold or makes one more likely to catch a cold.

BUSTED!

MOST SCIENTISTS AGREE THAT GOING OUTSIDE WITH WET HAIR WON'T MAKE YOU MORE LIKELY TO CATCH A COLD.

Scientists have known for a long time that viruses, teeny-tiny germs, cause colds. In fact, some cold viruses actually prefer drier conditions—in your nose and the air, that is, not in your hair. Heated homes and dry, chilly winter air can dry out the lining of your nose, making it a more appealing home for such viruses. This may explain why people get colds more often during the cooler months. Some scientists say the seasonal spike could also be due to an increase in germ swapping as people crowd together indoors.

Every year in the United States, 22 MILLION DAYS of school are missed because of a cold.

A WATCHED POT NEVER BOILS.

ORIGIN

Repeatedly looking at water while waiting for it to boil can make it seem like each stolen glance is prolonging things. A quick look and, oops, you just set the boil back by five seconds.

BUSTED!

NO MATTER HOW MUCH YOU LOOK AT IT, WATER WILL COME TO A BOIL WHEN IT'S GOOD AND READY. At sea level, this happens when (fresh) water reaches 212°F (100°C). At higher elevations, water boils at a lower temperature. For example, in Denver, Colorado, U.S.A., "the mile-high city," water boils when it reaches about 203°F (95°C). Below sea level, water boils at temperatures above 212°F. If you tried to make macaroni and cheese at the Dead Sea—minus 1,385 feet (-422 m) in elevation—you'd have to wait for the pot of water to reach about 215°F (102°C).

Water on Mars BOILS at 50°F (10°C).

29

MYTH

YOU SHOULD SMEAR BURNS WITH BUTTER.

ORIGIN

In the 1882 book *First Aid to the Injured: Five Ambulance Lectures,* a German surgeon gave this advice for treating burns: "Compresses of cold water generally increase the suffering. A covering of grease, oil, or some dry substance is far more soothing, and generally alleviates the pain more rapidly. You should therefore anoint the wound well with oil (lamp-oil, salad-oil, castor-oil, or any at hand); or paint it over with grease, lard, butter . . ."

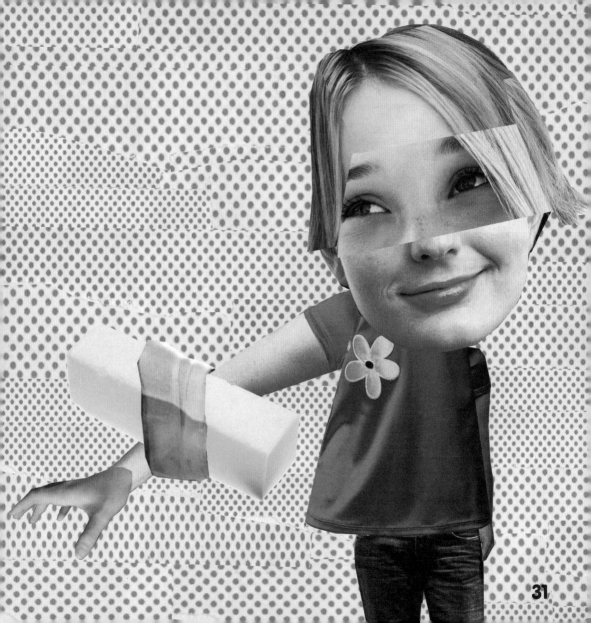

BUSTED!

SCIENTISTS TODAY HAVE SHOWN THAT RUNNING COOL WATER FOR 20 MINUTES OVER A BURN IS THE BEST TREATMENT.

Water flushes out the wound, cleaning it and making it less likely to become infected. It can also help ease pain, reduce swelling, and even speed up healing and lessen scarring. Butter can increase the likelihood of infection by trapping and introducing bacteria. Be sure not to ice a burn either, since this could also further damage the wound.

A sculpture made entirely of butter is unveiled every year at the Pennsylvania Farm Show. In 2013, Jim Victor shaped 1,000 POUNDS (454 KG) OF BUTTER into a scene depicting dairy products, fruits, vegetables, and Christmas trees.

ROOSTERS CROW ONLY AT DAWN.

ORIGIN

Like humans, roosters are diurnal, or active mostly during the daytime.
The birds often start their day with a *cock-a-doodle-do* . . . or two.

35

WHEN DOES A ROOSTER, OR MALE CHICKEN, CROW?

Whenever it wants. A rooster crows to scare off rival roosters. It crows when it senses a predator, or to communicate other things to its flock of hens. A rooster can be triggered to crow at any time of day or night, for many different reasons. Still not convinced? Get a pet rooster and find out for yourself the hard way.

The popular condiment nicknamed "ROOSTER SAUCE," for the bird that appears on some bottles, is actually *sriracha*, a hot sauce made from chili peppers, garlic, and vinegar.

37

URINE IS THE BEST TREATMENT FOR JELLYFISH STINGS.

ORIGIN

Hot water and seawater are recommended for some jellyfish stings. Urine, which contains salt, is also hot—roughly 100°F (38°C)—so the idea is not too far-fetched.

BUSTED!

THERE IS NO ONE WAY TO TREAT A JELLYFISH STING. THE BEST METHOD DEPENDS ON THE TYPE OF JELLYFISH.

Because some jellyfish are transparent or have long tentacles, people often don't see what stung them. But trained first responders will know best what jellyfish are in the area and how to react. Common treatments include seawater, vinegar, and hot water—but not urine! There is no scientific evidence that urine eases the pain of a sting or stops the stinging. And with seawater so nearby after a sting, there really is no good reason to pee on someone who's already in pain.

A jellyfish sting is delivered by nematocysts. When fired, these TINY, COILED STRUCTURES unwind and shoot like harpoons into the skin, delivering a painful toxin.

RUBBER TIRES AND RUBBER SHOE SOLES PROVIDE PROTECTION FROM LIGHTNING.

ORIGIN

Rubber is an insulator, a material that does not conduct, or transmit, electricity very well. And lightning scientists agree that generally you're safer inside a car than outside one.

BUSTED!

A FEW INCHES OF RUBBER IS SIMPLY NO MATCH FOR LIGHTNING. A BOLT DELIVERS TOO MUCH POWER TO BE STOPPED BY THE MATERIAL. And National Oceanic and Atmospheric Administration (NOAA) lightning safety expert John Jensenius points out, "Even if shoe soles did provide protection, lightning can jump gaps, between your ankle and the ground." Cars, however, do offer some protection, but not because of their tires. "Lightning often passes through tires themselves and causes them to pop," says Jensenius. Instead, he explains, "The metal shell of a car is what's providing protection. In general, lightning will travel around the car, in the frame." As long as you remain completely inside the car and avoid touching any metal, lightning that strikes a car will run through the metal surrounding you, not through you

You can estimate how far away from you a storm is by counting the amount of TIME BETWEEN THE FLASH OF THE LIGHTNING AND THE RUMBLE OF THE THUNDER. Each five seconds that passes between the two equals about one mile (1.6 km).

MORE
SHOCKING
MYTHS ABOUT
LIGHTNING

It's IMPOSSIBLE to be struck by lightning while indoors.

Although you're generally safer inside, lightning can still strike you there. Stay away from objects connected with the outside, such as corded phones and plumbing. Lightning can also travel through the electrical wires in your home, so you don't want to touch anything plugged into an electrical outlet.

If STUCK OUTSIDE during a storm, the best thing to do is stand under a tree, or lie flat on the ground.

Trees, because of their height, are more likely to get struck. If you're underneath one that's hit, the lightning could jump from the tree to you on its way to the ground. Lying flat on the ground puts you more at risk of being struck by the ground current that is created by lightning.

METAL attracts lightning.

Height, not material, is the biggest factor. Tall objects are more likely to be struck.

Lightning can't strike in a place where it's NOT RAINING.

Not true: Lightning can precede or follow a storm's precipitation.

If you touch a person who's been STRUCK BY LIGHTNING, you'll be electrocuted.

It is perfectly safe to help a lightning victim. The human body does not hold a charge.

HEAT LIGHTNING isn't real lightning.

It is real—real far away, and that's why you can see the light, but not hear the thunder.

47

MYTH

EATING CARROTS WILL IMPROVE YOUR EYESIGHT.

ORIGIN

There's a surprising story behind this myth. During World War II, the British military started a lie: They reported that the Royal Air Force's best pilots had amazing night vision thanks to a diet rich in carrots. Why lie? The British had a real, secret weapon—a radar—that was helping their pilots. But they wanted to keep it hidden from their enemies, the Nazis. So the Brits made up the story about the carrots to throw the Nazis off the truth. The public—not just the Nazis—got wind of the carrot claim, and a myth was born.

BUSTED!

THERE IS SOME TRUTH BEHIND
THIS MYTH.
Carrots are a good source of vitamin A, which is important for healthy sight. People with too little vitamin A in their diet can have trouble seeing at night or can even go blind. Increased vitamin A intake can improve these problems. But people with a well-rounded diet don't have a vitamin A deficiency. So chowing down on carrots won't correct their need to wear glasses, or any other vision problems they might have. And an abundance of carrots can't give anyone x-ray vision, superhuman night vision, or any other supersight. If you're still tempted to overload on carrots, consider this: Too much vitamin A can cause nausea and blurred vision and even turn your skin orange.

The world's longest carrot, grown in 2007, MEASURED 19 FEET 1.96 INCHES (5.841 M). That's a lot of vitamin A.

51

MYTH

YOU CAN CATCH A BIRD BY SPRINKLING SALT ON ITS TAIL.

ORIGIN

In 1580, English author John Lyly wrote: "It is . . . a foolish bird that stayeth the laying salt on hir taile." Today, the advice that you can catch a bird with the seasoning is often given to children—but as a joke!

53

People commonly think of salt and pepper as spices. And while pepper is indeed a spice, or a seasoning that comes from a plant, SALT IS NOT—IT'S A MINERAL.

BUSTED!

SALT DOESN'T RENDER A BIRD UNABLE TO FLY.

And even if it did, if you're close enough to a bird to sprinkle salt on its tail, you're probably close enough to catch it without the salt. But, in reality, a bird is pretty hard to catch with only your bare hands. Bird scientists like David Bonter at the Cornell Lab of Ornithology don't rely on a sneak attack with salt to catch birds for research. Instead, he says, "the most common method for catching birds is the mist net, a really fine black nylon mesh." Placed against a background of vegetation, the net is concealed enough that visiting birds fly into it, are cradled inside, and eventually plucked out by trained researchers. Bonter notes that "In North America, most birds are protected and you aren't allowed to catch them unless you have special permits and licenses. Without these, it's actually illegal to capture and hold wild birds." But, he adds, it is legal to take a hurt bird that you've found to a wildlife rehabilitation center.

MORE BIRD MYTHS

FEEDING BIRDS PREVENTS THEM FROM MIGRATING.
Feed freely. Bird migration is triggered by several factors. Whether you leave any seed out isn't one of them.

MOTHER BIRDS PUSH THEIR YOUNG OUT OF THE NEST WHEN IT'S TIME FOR THEM TO LEAVE.
Mama birds don't purposely push their babies out of the nest. Chicks fly when they're ready.

BROWN PELICANS GO BLIND FROM REPEATEDLY DIVING INTO THE WATER.
Adaptations protect pelican eyes from taking a beating each dip.

MYTH

THE TONGUE IS THE STRONGEST MUSCLE IN THE BODY.

ORIGIN
Scientists agree that the tongue is mighty, but is it the mightiest of all?

58

BUSTED!

THERE ISN'T A FIRM ANSWER TO THE QUESTION

"Which muscle in the body is the strongest?" There are several reasons for this. "Strongest" could mean a few different things. Is it the muscle that can exert the most force, or push or pull on another object? Is it the muscle that can make a repeated motion for the longest period of time? Or is it just the largest muscle? Things are further complicated by the fact that muscles don't act alone. If you look at a drawing of the muscles in the human body, you'll quickly notice how interconnected they are. Considering all of this, scientists say there are actually a few candidates for the strongest muscle, including the gluteus maximus (butt), masseter (jaw), and soleus (calf muscle).

Crocodiles can't STICK OUT THEIR TONGUES—they're attached to the bottom of their mouths!

MYTH

TOMATOES ARE THE BEST WAY TO GET RID OF SKUNK SMELL ON A DOG.

ORIGIN

People have rubbed everything from chopped tomatoes to tomato juice to ketchup on their pooches because this seems to get rid of the scent of skunk spray.

BUSTED!

YOU START SMELLING THE TOMATOES

INSTEAD OF THE SPRAY BECAUSE OF SOMETHING CALLED OLFACTORY FATIGUE.
Your nose (the olfactory part) shuts down (the fatigue part) when bombarded by skunk smell. "The nose stops smelling it, and if tomato juice is present, you could smell that instead of the skunk spray," explains Humboldt State University chemist William Wood, who has studied skunk spray for years. Substances called thiols are responsible for the spray's stink. To neutralize, or truly get rid of, the odor, you need to change the thiols into other molecules. Tomatoes can't do this. Other substances can, thankfully. See the following pages for a do-it-yourself recipe, concocted by chemist Paul Krebaum and recommended by the Humane Society.

SKUNK SPRAY IS FLAMMABLE— this means it catches fire when lit!

MAKE YOUR OWN
SKUNK-SMELL REMEDY

IT'S BEST TO MAKE THIS RECIPE WITH AN ADULT'S HELP OR SUPERVISION. Be sure to wear rubber gloves during the mixing and the washing.

MIX

- 1 QUART OF 3% HYDROGEN PEROXIDE
- ¼ CUP BAKING SODA
- 1 TEASPOON LIQUID DISHWASHING SOAP

Wash your skunked dog with this mixture as soon as possible. Be sure to keep the mixture away from the dog's eyes. Rub the mixture into the dog's fur for about five minutes and then rinse thoroughly. Don't leave the mixture on the dog for a long time, since the ingredients can bleach fur. Wash your pooch with pet shampoo and rinse again.

CAUTION!

This mixture could explode if left in a bottle. So when you're done, don't save it, throw it away. Also, don't make it ahead of time.

MYTH

THE LOST CITY OF
ATLANTIS
IS BURIED
UNDERWATER.

ORIGIN

In 360 B.C., the ancient Greek philosopher and author Plato wrote "there was an island situated in front of the straits which are by you called the Pillars of Heracles; the island was larger than Libya and Asia put together . . . Now in this island of Atlantis there was a great and wonderful empire which had rule over the whole island and several others, and over parts of the continent . . . in a single day and night of misfortune all your warlike men in a body sank into the earth, and the island of Atlantis in like manner disappeared in the depths of the sea."

BUSTED!

OVER THE YEARS, PEOPLE HAVE CLAIMED TO HAVE FOUND ATLANTIS.

But most scientists agree that there isn't enough evidence to say that Atlantis has been found—or that it even ever existed. "It really is nothing more than a myth—you really get that if you sit down and read Plato," says New York State Museum archaeologist Charles Orser. When it comes to speculation about its location, "Atlantis has been everywhere," he says. "The funniest place is that it's under the ice in Antarctica." What would it take to convince the majority of archaeologists that Atlantis is real? "Some really careful excavation, probably in the Mediterranean or somewhere thereabouts, that would reveal elements mentioned by Plato: the circular canals, the strange metal, the racecourse. And that would be extremely expensive and difficult to do," explains Orser. He cautions that while instruments used aboveground can detect something below the surface (think metal detectors), "sometimes when you dig, there's nothing there."

Twelve out of every ONE MILLION BABIES BORN in the U.S. in 2013 were named Atlantis.

MORE
MYTHOLOGICAL
PLACES

EL DORADO, AN EMPIRE OF GOLD IN THE JUNGLES OF SOUTH AMERICA

UTOPIA, A REMOTE PLACE OF PERFECTION

CAMELOT, SITE OF KING ARTHUR'S PALACE AND COURT ON THE ISLAND OF GREAT BRITAIN

SOAKED FINGERS WRINKLE BECAUSE THEY'RE ABSORBING WATER.

ORIGIN

Scientists used to believe that a process called osmosis was behind the wrinkles. Osmosis is the movement of a solvent—in this case, water—from a less concentrated area to a more concentrated area. They thought that water in a bathtub or pool seeping into the outer layer of skin caused it to swell, and eventually wrinkle.

BUSTED!

SCIENTISTS NOW KNOW THAT OSMOSIS IS NOT THE CAUSE OF PRUNEY FINGERS.

Instead, the wrinkling is triggered by the body's nervous system. This network of nerves allows the brain and other parts of the body to "talk" to each other. Nerves tell blood vessels in soaked fingers to narrow. This reduces blood flow to the fingers, which causes them to lose volume—in a sense, deflate—and wrinkle. So how did scientists figure this out? They conducted studies and observed that fingers with nerve damage—including severed fingers that had been reattached—don't wrinkle when immersed in water!

In a recent study, people with soaked, WRINKLED FINGERS moved wet objects from one container to another faster than people with dry fingers. The finding suggests that our fingers may wrinkle because the folds help us hold on to wet objects.

69

DOLPHINS ARE A DETERRENT TO SHARKS.

ORIGIN

These two types of sea creatures aren't exactly best friends. So perhaps they've come to an agreement to stick to separate sides of the sea?

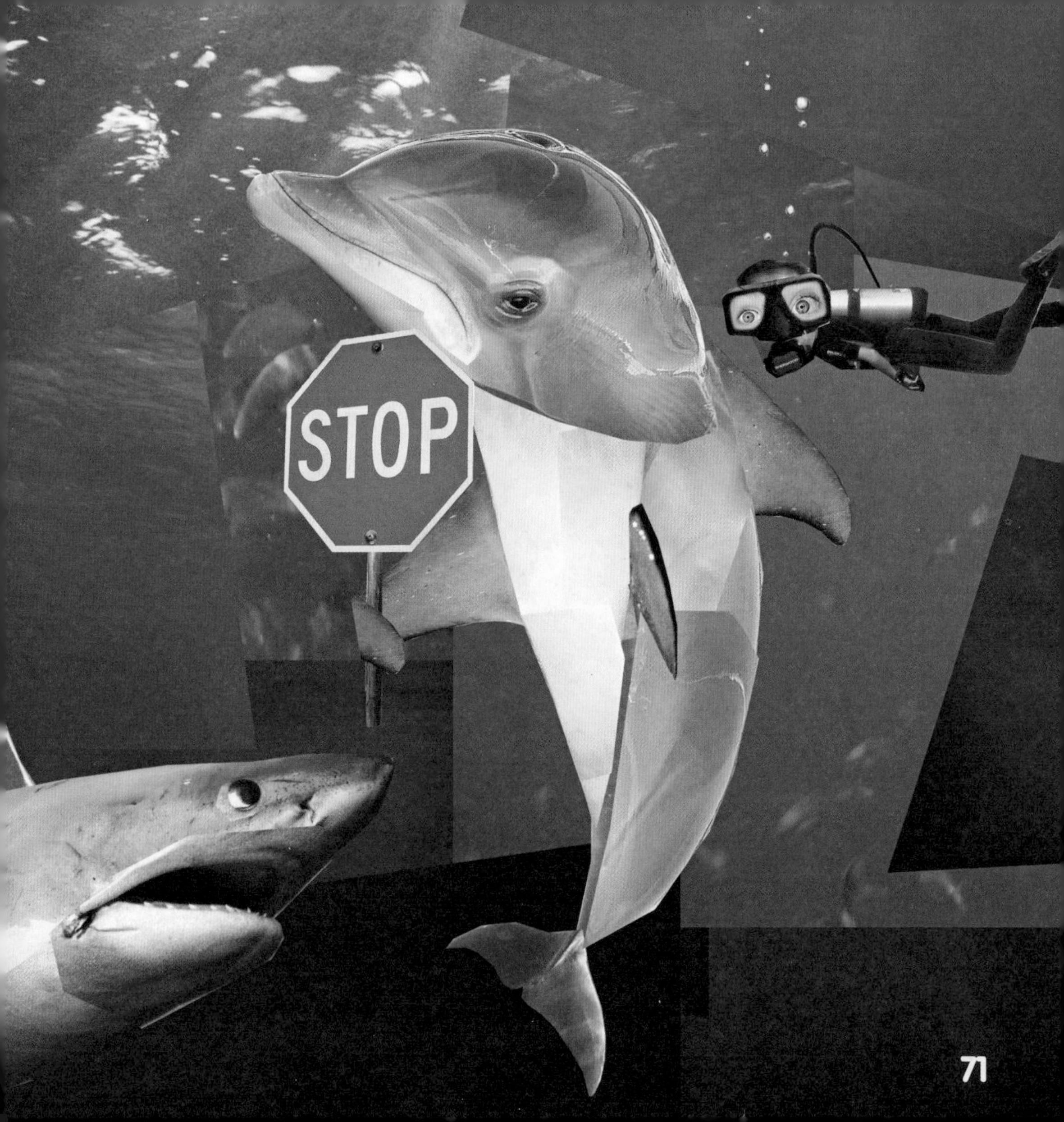
STOP

Orcas—or killer whales, as they are commonly known—ARE ACTUALLY DOLPHINS.

BUSTED!

IT'S NOT UNCOMMON FOR SHARKS AND DOLPHINS TO FIGHT AND PREY ON EACH OTHER. These encounters—and the resulting scars—are evidence that the two don't always avoid each other. So where there are dolphins, there are also sharks. Also, scientists point out, a large school of fish will attract both fearsome sharks and friendly dolphins to feed.

MORE SHARK MYTHS

SHARK BRAINS ARE THE SIZE OF A WALNUT. There is no standard brain size for sharks. The size varies by species. But some brains are several feet long— significantly larger than a walnut.

SHARKS CAN REGROW FINS IF THEY ARE CUT OFF. Sadly, they can't. They sink to the seafloor and die.

SHARKS NEVER ATTACK HUMANS AT MIDDAY. Shark attacks, while rare, happen at all times, including the afternoon, records show.

ALL SHARKS MUST CONSTANTLY SWIM IN ORDER TO BREATHE. Some sharks have ways to keep water moving over their gills while at rest.

SHARKS HAVE NO PREDATORS. People, parasites, and other sharks kill sharks.

VIKING WARRIORS
WORE HORNED HELMETS.

ORIGIN

By the late 1800s, illustrations of Vikings almost always showed them wearing a helmet with horns. This historical inaccuracy is likely the result of some cultural confusion.

BUSTED!

IN THE 1800S, ARCHAEOLOGISTS AT SEVERAL SITES IN EUROPE UNEARTHED ARTIFACTS DEPICTING HORNED HEADGEAR. Those artifacts are too old to have belonged to the Vikings, a northern European, seafaring people who first appeared in the eighth century. And experts say evidence shows that real Viking warriors did not wear horned helmets. But the headgear of those other ancient European cultures inspired the idea of a Viking in a horned helmet, and the image stuck. Today, it can be found in everything from the movie *How to Train Your Dragon* to the comic strip "Hägar the Horrible," and the mascot of the NFL football team the Minnesota Vikings is—you guessed it—a Viking in a horned helmet.

The Vikings were the first Europeans to explore North America. More than a THOUSAND YEARS AGO, they set sail from Greenland and settled at a site in what is now Newfoundland, Canada.

EATING CHOCOLATE GIVES YOU PIMPLES.

ORIGIN

This idea has been around for nearly a century, and cultures around the world believe diet can affect skin health.

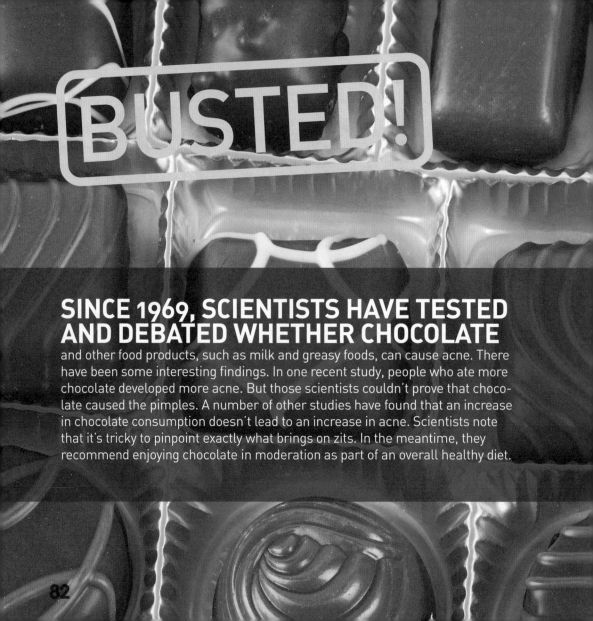

BUSTED!

SINCE 1969, SCIENTISTS HAVE TESTED AND DEBATED WHETHER CHOCOLATE

and other food products, such as milk and greasy foods, can cause acne. There have been some interesting findings. In one recent study, people who ate more chocolate developed more acne. But those scientists couldn't prove that chocolate caused the pimples. A number of other studies have found that an increase in chocolate consumption doesn't lead to an increase in acne. Scientists note that it's tricky to pinpoint exactly what brings on zits. In the meantime, they recommend enjoying chocolate in moderation as part of an overall healthy diet.

The world's LARGEST CHOCOLATE BAR was created in 2011 and weighed 12,770 pounds 4.48 ounces (5,792.1 kg). That's nearly the weight of an adult male African elephant!

83

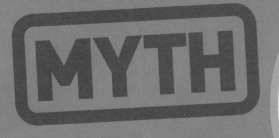

MYTH

BANANAS GROW ON TREES.

ORIGIN
The plants the fruits grow on certainly *look* like trees!

BUSTED!

THAT'S NO BANANA TREE—that's a banana herb. Other herbs include mint, basil, oregano, and strawberry, to name a few. Technically, trees have woody stems; think of the bark on trunks. Herbs like bananas don't have this. But banana plants do grow as big as a tree—in fact, they're the world's largest herb.

Though in America KETCHUP is commonly made from tomatoes, in fact, the condiment can be made from all sorts of things, like mushrooms, walnuts, and—popular in the Philippines—bananas.

85

MYTH

CRACKING YOUR KNUCKLES WILL GIVE YOU ARTHRITIS IN YOUR HANDS.

ORIGIN

When knuckles are cracked, they make a popping noise that to some people sounds damaging.

BUSTED!

TURNS OUT THIS CLAIM ISN'T ALL IT'S CRACKED UP TO BE.
Studies have repeatedly found that kn cracking does not make someone more likely to get arthritis in their hands. Art a common condition that causes pain and stiffness in the joints. Found where p your skeleton connect, or join, joints allow you to crack your knuckles, wave yo bend your elbow, swivel your head, and walk. That popping noise, it turns out, i harmless sound of bubbles becoming many more, smaller bubbles in the fluid joints. Even though arthritis can't be blamed on knuckle cracking, doctors still people to go easy on the habit: Studies have found that frequent knuckle crack in, a lot every day over decades—can weaken a person's grip and cause swelli

To test this myth, California doctor Donald Unger CRACKED HIS KNUCKLES on only one hand, his left, at least twice a day for 50 years but left the knuckles on his right hand alone. An examination of his hands after the experiment found that neither had developed arthritis, and there were no other differences detected between the two hands.

MYTH

DOGS SWEAT THROUGH THEIR TONGUE.

ORIGIN
This idea probably stems from the fact that hot dogs pant. Also, have you ever hugged a sweaty dog?

88

BUSTED!

DOGS DO SWEAT

—but only through their paw pads. Canines also cool off by panting, which releases body heat.

The world's longest dog tongue MEASURES 4.5 INCHES (11.43 CM). You might expect it to belong to a big pooch. But Puggy the Pekingese, a breed that on average weighs less than 14 pounds (6.35 kg), is the proud owner.

MORE
MYTHS ABOUT
YOUR
TONGUE

THE TIP OF YOUR TONGUE IS THE ONLY PLACE ON YOUR TONGUE THAT CAN TASTE SWEETNESS. Actually, you can taste sweetness all over your tongue.

ADAM'S APPLE

WISH BONE

FUNNY BONE

TYPE D BATTERIES (2 Required)

A "TONGUE-ROLLING" GENE DETERMINES WHETHER YOU CAN CURL UP THE SIDES OF YOUR TONGUE. Genetics alone can't curl your tongue. Studies have found that in pairs of identical twins, one twin sometimes can curl his or her tongue while the other can't.

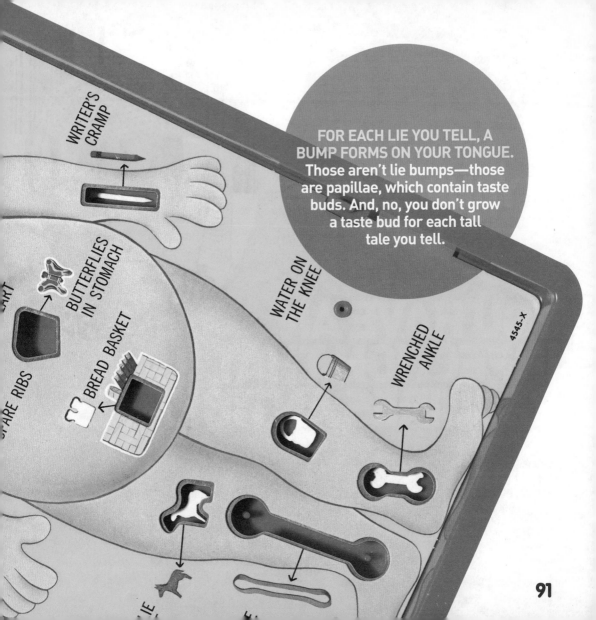

WRITER'S CRAMP

FOR EACH LIE YOU TELL, A BUMP FORMS ON YOUR TONGUE. Those aren't lie bumps—those are papillae, which contain taste buds. And, no, you don't grow a taste bud for each tall tale you tell.

BUTTERFLIES IN STOMACH

WATER ON THE KNEE

BREAD BASKET

WRENCHED ANKLE

ARE RIBS

4545-X

91

IF YOUR SNOT IS GREEN, YOU HAVE AN INFECTION THAT REQUIRES ANTIBIOTICS.

ORIGIN

The color green has been associated with illness for a very long time. The oldest written record of the connection dates to 1250, according to the Oxford English Dictionary. And the popular expression "green around the gills" has been used since the 1800s to describe a sick person's complexion. Also, an abundance of white blood cells sent by the body's immune system to fight germs in the nose can give snot a greenish hue.

BUSTED!

THERE ARE TWO TYPES OF INFECTIONS:

those caused by viruses and those caused by bacteria. Doctors prescribe antibiotics to fight bacterial infections only. Mucus color alone can't tell your doctor whether you have an infection and if so what type it is. People sick with viral infections, people sick with bacterial infections, and (less often) people sick with neither can have green snot. And sick people can have clear snot.

GUSTATORY RHINITIS is what doctors call a runny nose caused by eating spicy foods.

93

MORE COLOR MYTHS

BLUE IS THE COLOR OF BLOOD INSIDE THE HUMAN BODY. No—blood is red, both inside and outside of your body.

RED M&MS GIVE YOU CANCER. Relax—they don't. The scare stems from studies that reported red dye No. 2 might cause cancer. That dye was never used to color the candies.

"ORANGE" HAS NO WORD THAT RHYMES WITH IT. The little-known word "sporange"—which is the casing in which spores are formed in plants—rhymes with orange.

GREEN IS THE COLOR OF FULLY RIPE LIMES.
Yellow is a better bet for ripeness.

"BLUE MOONS" ARE ACTUALLY BLUE.
Blue moons have to do with frequency, not color. A blue moon is an extra full moon in a season or month.

PINK IS FOR GIRLS.
Pink is for boys, too. Just like blue isn't only for boys.

95

IF YOU CUT AN EARTHWORM IN HALF, IT WILL BECOME TWO SEPARATE EARTHWORMS.

ORIGIN

An earthworm can regrow its tail end if cut off. And fragments of other types of worms, microscopic wrigglers called planarians, can regrow heads!

97

BUSTED!

"ALL OF THE ESSENTIAL ORGANS IN EARTHWORMS ARE IN THE FIRST 40 TO 60 SEGMENTS, DEPENDING ON THE SPECIES," explains worm expert John Reynolds. So if you slice an earthworm behind these segments, somewhere in its hind end, the animal can regrow its tail. This ability to sprout a new body part is called regeneration. Some earthworms even "drop tail segments to escape predators," notes Reynolds. But, he says, sliced-off tails won't grow a head and become a new earthworm.

HOW DO YOU TELL WHICH END OF AN EARTHWORM IS THE HEAD? Earthworms sometimes have a clitellum, a band around the body that divides the front from the rear. The majority of the worm is the tail end. But since a clitellum isn't always present, the better bet is to look for the worm's prostomium. This fleshy lobe can be found over the mouth. It's used in feeding much like an elephant uses its trunk to eat.

MORE
ANIMALS
THAT CAN
GROW NEW
BODY PARTS

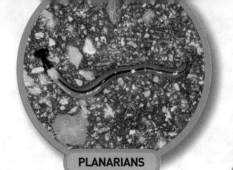

PLANARIANS

SEA STARS

SALAMANDERS AND NEWTS

LIZARDS

WALKING STICKS

ZEBRAFISH

LOBSTERS

MYTH

SHAVING HAIR MAKES IT GROW BACK THICKER.

ORIGIN

The rough growth that appears shortly after shaving—called stubble—feels thicker.
But is the hair actually thicker?

SHAVING DOESN'T CHANGE HOW HAIR GROWS.

Since the 1920s, studies have shown that shaved hair on the face, legs, and other body parts doesn't grow back thicker—or darker or faster. Hair that grows back after shaving feels thicker only at first. That's because when you shave, you're cutting off the part of the hair that's been above the skin and become weathered—softer, tapered at the tips—with time. Shaving leaves the shaft of hair with a blunt tip that feels thicker. But if left to grow out fully, hair will eventually feel like it did before it was shaved.

The average human hair is about 100 MICROMETERS THICK, about the same thickness as a sheet of copy paper.

MYTH

CAFFEINE STUNTS YOUR GROWTH.

ORIGIN

An old study on the elderly linked lots of caffeine—a substance found in coffee, soda, energy drinks, tea, and chocolate—with osteoporosis, a disease that weakens bones.

BUSTED!

THERE ARE OTHER EXPLANATIONS FOR WHY THE PARTICIPANTS IN THE EARLY STUDY HAD OSTEOPOROSIS. And more recent research hasn't turned up any evidence that caffeine will keep a kid from growing. But you should monitor your caffeine intake anyway. That's because caffeine is a stimulant, or a type of drug that puts some pep in your step. Most people consume it when they want to be more alert. But too much caffeine can give you the jitters and cause problems like an upset stomach or trouble sleeping.

People pay a lot of money for Kopi Luwak coffee— even though its beans were PLUCKED FROM THE POOP of a civet, a catlike mammal!

107

HIGHWAY OVERPASSES
PROTECT
YOU FROM
TORNADOES.

ORIGIN

On April 10, 1979, a Texas man crawled up under a highway overpass to escape the destructive wind and debris of a passing tornado. He lived to tell the tale in a documentary. Then, in April 1991, a news crew hiding beneath a Kansas highway overpass famously filmed a tornado as it roared by.

On March 12, 2006, a Missouri tornado sucked a 19-year-old out of his mobile home and carried the unconscious teen 1,307 feet (398 m) to a nearby field, where he awoke with only minor injuries. The teenager traveled more than TEN TIMES THE DISTANCE THE WRIGHT BROTHERS FLEW DURING THEIR FIRST FLIGHT, IN 1903.

BUSTED!

WEATHER AND SAFETY OFFICIALS STRESS THAT PEOPLE SHOULD NOT SEEK SHELTER FROM TORNADOES UNDER HIGHWAY OVERPASSES. These structures—essentially bridges over highways—form a wedge where the bridge meets the ground or concrete as it slopes down toward the highway below. People sometimes believe that crawling up the slope and tucking into the space underneath the bridge offers some sort of protection, when instead it almost always does not. Experts say the safest place to be during a tornado is in a basement or in an interior room on the lowest floor, and beneath a mattress, if possible, to help protect against flying debris. If caught out in the open, get out of your car and lie down in the lowest place possible, such as a ditch. Getting down low is important because tornado winds are weaker at ground level. So, in fact, climbing up into an overpass exposes you to stronger winds that funnel debris beneath the structure. People have died seeking shelter beneath highway overpasses. Those that survived, as in the 1979 and 1991 videos (see origin), were lucky.

A PERSON CAN SURVIVE AN ELEVATOR DROP BY JUMPING JUST BEFORE THE ELEVATOR HITS THE BOTTOM.

ORIGIN

Some people reason that if they were midair when the elevator crashed into the ground, they would avoid the impact and land safely on their feet.

113

BUSTED!

TO COUNTER THE IMPACT OF THE CRASH, YOU'D HAVE TO JUMP UP AT ABOUT THE SAME SPEED THAT THE ELEVATOR CRASHES INTO THE GROUND. If it hits at 30 miles (48.3 km) an hour, that's 44 feet (13.4 m) a second. Can you jump up that fast, and at precisely the right moment? No way. But here's some reassuring news: Elevators are held by multiple cables, not just one. So a single snap wouldn't send you plummeting. And several things, including brakes activated during a drop, would help cushion a fall.

Repeatedly PRESSING THE CALL BUTTON FOR AN ELEVATOR will not make it arrive quicker. Also, pressing the "door close" button may make the doors start to close sooner, but it can't increase the speed at which they close.

MYTH

A BUTTERED PIECE OF TOAST ALWAYS LANDS FACEDOWN ON THE BUTTERED SIDE.

ORIGIN
Popular belief holds that the buttered side of the bread is heavier and therefore ends up facedown after a fall.

BUSTED!

HOW A BUTTERED PIECE OF TOAST WILL LAND HAS NOTHING TO DO WITH THE BUTTER: There's too little of it and it's spread too thinly to make a difference in how the toast tumbles. How the toast lands depends on many different things, such as the shape and height of the table or plate the toast fell from, and the type of tumble the toast took—did it skid off of or gently slip from a surface, was it first flung upward into the air, did it bounce? Several experiments have investigated the matter. One found that buttered toast landed buttered side down close to half of the time it fell from a table, and noted that the size of the table's overhang helped determine how the toast landed. Another study, though, found that toast most often lands buttered side down, largely because of the height from which it is most likely to fall: table or waist height. That study's author, Robert Matthews, found that such short heights don't give toast time to rotate midair from faceup (as on a plate) to facedown and back to faceup. Matthews' suggestion for saving your breakfast? "Toast seen heading off the table should be given a smart swipe forward with the hand," and "a plate off which toast is sliding should be moved swiftly downwards and backwards."

In 2012, a piece of toast left over from Prince Charles' breakfast the day he married Lady Diana Spencer—July 29, 1981—WAS AUCTIONED OFF FOR $360.

MYTH

RHINOCEROSES PUT OUT FIRES IN THE WILD.

ORIGIN
According to a Southeast Asian legend, rhinos stomp out fires in the forest.

BUSTED!

RHINOS SOMETIMES STOMP—but not on fires. There is no record of rhinos putting out fires in the wild, as heroic as that would be. Like other animals, rhinos instinctively run away from fire.

The word rhinoceros means "NOSE HORN" in Greek.

MYTH

DIET COKE AND MENTOS EATEN TOGETHER WILL EXPLODE IN YOUR STOMACH.

ORIGIN

A popular science experiment in which Mentos candies are dropped into a two-liter bottle of Diet Coke does create an awesome vertical explosion of fizz. The idea that combining the two things in a person's stomach would make them explode traces to an urban myth that circulated on the Internet about a little boy in Brazil who died after doing so.

123

BUSTED!

On October 17, 2010, 2,865 FIZZY FOUNTAINS OF SODA ERUPTED in a mall in the Philippines, when the world record was set for most geysers created by dropping Mentos into soda bottles.

A BIG BURP IS THE ONLY EXPLOSION YOU'LL EXPERIENCE IF YOU EAT MENTOS AND DRINK COKE TOGETHER.

When Mentos are dropped into a soda bottle, the carbon dioxide inside the soda crowds the surface of the candies. This creates a buildup of bubbles that shoves the soda out of the opening at the top. But carbon dioxide can collect on many more surfaces in your mouth. So not all of that gas ends up in your gut. And even if it did, your body provides a nice, big exit point: your mouth.

125

YOU SHOULD RUN IN A ZIGZAG TO ESCAPE A PURSUING CROCODILE.

ORIGIN

Crocs have long bodies. Their shape doesn't seem well suited for making repeated sharp turns while running.

CROCODILE ESCAPE ROUTE

BUSTED!

CROCS ATTACK IN A SINGLE, POWERFUL LUNGE FROM WATER, NOT BY CHASING PREY OVER LAND.

They prefer the element of surprise, lying in wait in the water and then springing forward and snapping their jaws around an animal. That's because they can't move rapidly on land and tire quickly there. Some crocs do gallop (imagine a rabbit on the go) but not very fast, and not toward something typically, but rather away from it and back to the water, where the croc feels safer. Croc scientists advise that if you do find yourself on land with a croc in hot pursuit, run in a straight line, which allows you to run faster and cover more ground.

Crocs have been clocked galloping at about **11 MILES AN HOUR (18 KM/H)**.

MYTH

IT'S IMPOSSIBLE TO FOLD PAPER IN HALF MORE THAN SEVEN TIMES.

ORIGIN

Try folding any piece of paper in half repeatedly and you'll find that it quickly becomes thicker than it is long, which makes the paper difficult to bend.

paper FOLDING Championship

131

BUSTED!

IN 2002, HIGH SCHOOL STUDENT BRITNEY GALLIVAN FAMOUSLY FOLDED A SHEET OF PAPER IN HALF 12 TIMES, setting a new world record. The clever teenager calculated the size of paper needed to disprove the myth and then folded an unspooled roll of toilet paper in half a dozen times.

The longest flight ever
made by a piece of paper
folded into an airplane
and launched by hand is
27.9 SECONDS.

BEARS
CAN'T RUN DOWNHILL.

ORIGIN

A bear is a big animal, weighing anywhere from hundreds to more than 1,000 pounds (454 kg). It may seem like all that bulk would quickly make a bear running downhill roll downhill instead.

BUSTED!

A BEAR CAN RUN DOWNHILL, YOU BETTER BELIEVE IT. And a
bear can run pretty fast. How fast? Faster than you—more
than 30 miles an hour (48 km/h). Because of this, bear
experts advise that you never run away from a charging
bear and instead stand your ground.

MALE BEARS ARE CALLED BOARS, FEMALE BEARS SOWS—the same names used for male pigs and female pigs.

MORE
BEAR
MYTHS

THE POLAR BEAR
IS THE ONLY TYPE OF BEAR
THAT CAN SWIM.
Other types of bears can
swim, and quite well.

BEARS HAVE
POOR EYESIGHT.
Sure, they're excellent
sniffers, but they
can see too!

A BEAR STANDING
ON ITS HIND LEGS IS
ABOUT TO CHARGE.
Most likely, it's just curious
and standing up to get a
better look or sniff.

POLAR BEARS
ARE LEFT-HANDED.
No, they're right-handed.
Just kidding—they
don't seem to have a
preference.

GIANT PANDAS ARE
MORE CLOSELY RELATED TO
RACCOONS THAN TO BEARS.
Giant pandas are considered
true bears and so are more
closely related to other
bears than to raccoons.

BLACK BEARS "HOOT."
Scientists have no support
for this claim. Some believe
this sound may actually
be made by a porcupine,
not a bear!

YOU LOSE MOST OF YOUR BODY HEAT THROUGH YOUR HEAD.

ORIGIN

Decades-old misinterpreted military experiments are behind this myth, which is still repeated in everything from survival guides to winter weather warnings.

BUSTED!

Your BODY SHIVERS when cold to generate heat.

IF YOU LOSE MOST OF YOUR BODY HEAT THROUGH YOUR HEAD, it's only because you forgot to put on a hat but are otherwise fully clothed. How much heat a body part loses depends mostly on how big that body part is. Find a full-length mirror. Does your head take up more space than your legs? If so, you have bigger problems than heat loss. The bottom line is that it's a good idea to cover your head when it's cold, of course—just like it's a good idea to wear pants when it's cold.

YOU SHOULD LEAVE A WINDOW OPEN DURING A HURRICANE.

ORIGIN

Hurricanes and tornadoes are examples of low-pressure systems. As they pass by a house, the difference between the air pressure inside and outside increases. Scientists used to believe that this difference could grow great enough to blow the roof off a house. (Think about when your ears pop during a flight. This happens because the pressure inside them becomes much greater than the pressure outside them.) People thought that opening a window would relieve that difference, by letting air molecules flow more freely between the inside and outside.

144

145

BUSTED!

NOAA HURRICANE EXPERT NEAL DORST SAYS THAT THE AIR PRESSURE DIFFER-ENCE INSIDE AND OUTSIDE A HOME—even one without any windows open— never gets big enough to cause an explosion. So you don't need to leave a window open. In fact, it's a terrible idea: It lets in high winds and debris that could harm anyone inside and seriously damage a home—including ripping the roof off, which then makes the house much more likely to collapse, or look like it exploded. Experts say to instead close all windows and cover them with storm shutters.

There are NO HURRICANE NAMES that begin with the letters Q, U, X, Y, or Z.

OFFICIAL ATLANTIC HURRICANE NAMES FOR 2014

ARTHUR
BERTHA
CRISTOBAL
DOLLY
EDOUARD
FAY

GONZALO
HANNA
ISAIAS
JOSEPHINE
KYLE
LAURA

MARCO
NANA
OMAR
PAULETTE
RENE
SALLY
TEDDY
VICKY
WILFRED

149

HANGING A PLASTIC BAG OF WATER REPELS FLIES.

ORIGIN

There are several theories out there for why this would work. One says that looking at the bags overwhelms fly eyes and disorients the insects. Another swears that prisms created by the bags scare flies. Still another claims that flies freak out when they see their distorted reflection in the bags.

BUSTED!

THESE EXPLANATIONS "HOLD NO WATER," says

Philip Kaufman, an insect scientist and expert on fly control at the University of Florida. Cole Gilbert, an expert on fly sight at Cornell University, agrees: "I can't think of a reason why this practice would work." Indeed, there's no scientific evidence that the bags repel flies. A test performed by another fly scientist found that the bags were useless. So what does help keep out flies? Screen doors and positioning dumpsters far from them, Kaufman says.

Houseflies LAY THEIR EGGS IN POOP and garbage so that their young have something to eat when they hatch. When they do hatch, they spend most of their time buried headfirst in their food, and breathe through their hind end.

MYTH

MICE LOVE CHEESE.

ORIGIN

This myth might stem from the popular saying "quiet as a mouse." More than 300 years ago, that meant to be as quiet as a mouse in cheese—in other words, to make a soft, muffled sound.

MMM, MICE DO LOVE CHEESE.

And chocolate. And peanut butter. And seeds. And fruit. Mice will eat most anything they can get their paws on. But studies haven't found the rodents prefer cheese to all other food. In fact, pest control experts typically use foods other than cheese to entice mice into traps.

The word "mouse" was first used to DESCRIBE A HAND-HELD DEVICE used with computers in 1965.

155

MYTH

AIRPLANES GET RID OF TOILET WASTE BY DUMPING IT WHILE MIDAIR.

ORIGIN

The strong suctioning sound an airplane toilet makes when you flush it makes it seem like waste is being whisked away outside the craft. Reports of stinky, dark-colored fluids falling from the skies contribute to the myth, too.

BUSTED!

The feces of astronauts aboard the International Space Station are stored and then whisked away with other waste by an unmanned spacecraft. IT BURNS UP UPON REENTERING EARTH'S ATMOSPHERE. Urine is recycled and used for drinking water.

IT'S HIGHLY LIKELY THAT A BIRD, NOT A PLANE, LET LOOSE THAT POOP FROM ABOVE. A pilot can't release a plane's toilet tank contents. Only someone operating a lever on the exterior of the plane can do that. The tank is emptied when a plane is grounded, not while midair. The Federal Aviation Administration, or FAA, reports that calls complaining of waste from the sky increase in the fall—around the same time birds resume their migration, often in large groups. Investigations by the FAA and the Environmental Protection Agency have found that virtually all of the brown droplets suspected to be from people are in fact from birds.

IF A GROUNDHOG SEES ITS SHADOW ON FEBRUARY 2, GROUNDHOG DAY, THERE WILL BE SIX MORE WEEKS OF WINTER.

ORIGIN

Immigrants from northern Europe brought the tradition to America. But it has even deeper roots, in Imbolc, the ancient Celtic celebration in early February that marked the first day of spring.

IF YOU THINK THERE'S SOMETHING SHADY ABOUT GROUND-HOG DAY, YOU'RE RIGHT. Studies show that the most famous weather-forecasting groundhog, Punxsutawney Phil, of Pennsylvania, can't really predict when spring will arrive. He's wrong more often than he's right. But give him a break: It's hard to predict the weather that far in advance. And Pennsylvania groundhogs do first emerge from hibernation close to their namesake day: February 4, on average, says biologist Stam Zervanos, of Pennsylvania State University Berks. But, he notes, they don't leave their hibernation holes for good then. They spend a few weeks finding each other and marking their territory. Then they return to their burrows for several more weeks of hibernation before finally emerging one last time in early March.

BUSTED!

In case you were wondering, GROUNDHOGS ARE ALSO CALLED WOODCHUCKS. They're the same thing.

OTHER
GROUNDHOGS
WHO GIVE WEATHER
FORECASTS
ON FEBRUARY 2

WIARTON WILLIE, OF
WIARTON, ONTARIO

JIMMY THE GROUNDHOG, OF
SUN PRAIRIE, WISCONSIN

STATEN ISLAND CHUCK, OF NEW YORK, NEW YORK

GENERAL BEAUREGARD LEE, OF ATLANTA, GEORGIA

SHUBENACADIE SAM, OF SHUBENACADIE, NOVA SCOTIA

SIR WALTER WALLY, OF RALEIGH, NORTH CAROLINA

MOSS GROWS ONLY ON THE NORTH SIDE OF TREES.

ORIGIN

Moss loves shade and moisture. The north face of a tree typically receives the least sunlight and so stays wet best. So an old rule of thumb for those lost in the woods is to find moss, and you'll have found north.

BUSTED!

IF YOU GET LOST IN THE WOODS, DON'T LOOK TO MOSS FOR HELP.
Moss can grow on any side of a tree, as long as it's shady and wet enough. Trees, branches, hills, or mountains can cast a shadow on a tree and create ideal conditions on its east, west, and south sides too. And keep in mind that the north face of a tree is its shadiest side only in the Northern Hemisphere. In the Southern Hemisphere, the south face of a tree typically receives the least sunlight.

Moss has been USED AS A PACKING MATERIAL for millennia. People have stuffed it in mattresses and fragile shipments, in the holes of a home's walls, and even around baby bottoms, as a diaper!

EARWIGS LIKE TO CRAWL INTO EARS.

ORIGIN

According to European superstition that's more than 1,000 years old, these insects—less than one inch (25 mm) in length—crawl into the ears of the fast asleep and then bore into their brains to lay eggs.

BUSTED!

EARWIGS DO LIKE MOIST, DARK PLACES, WHICH COULD DESCRIBE YOUR BRAIN. And these little critters are most active at night, when you're fast asleep. But they don't crawl into your ear and brain for sport or to lay eggs. In fact, they are no more likely than any other insect—that is, very unlikely—to crawl into your ear. Earwigs can give you a little pinch, though. Pincers on their hind end are used defensively as well as for capturing prey.

Used as a verb, "earwig" MEANS TO PESTER OR INFLUENCE SOMEONE through private conversation.

COYOTES AND WOLVES HOWL AT THE MOON.

ORIGIN

Canids—members of a family of animals that includes wolves, dogs, and coyotes—
have been mystically linked with the moon for millennia. The two appear in ancient
Native American, Norse, and Greek tales, among others.

173

BUSTED!

CANIDS AREN'T HOWLING AT THE MOON.

They're howling at each other. So what are they saying? "'Hey, I'm over here,' to another member of their group," says animal behavior scientist Marc Bekoff, of Project Coyote. "Or, it's territorial, to say to another pack, 'Hey, we're over here, this is our turf.'" They also howl to say hi and during play. The moon and its phase don't matter—canids howl even on new moon, or moonless, nights. And though it might seem like they howl more often at night, they can howl at any time of day—much like a rooster and its crow.

How can you tell the difference between a coyote howl and a wolf howl? They're similar, so it's tricky to tell them apart, especially when wolf pups join in. But an expert ear often can tell the two sounds apart. WOLVES, WHICH ARE BIGGER, PRODUCE A BIGGER, LOWER SOUND. COYOTES TEND TO HAVE MORE HIGH-PITCHED HOWLS, WITH YIPS MIXED IN.

LEFT-HANDED PEOPLE ARE MORE CREATIVE.

ORIGIN

Your brain is divided into two hemispheres, a right and a left. Generally, the right hemisphere is considered the more "creative" half, the left the more "logical." The right side of your brain controls muscle activity on the left side of your body, and vice versa. So, the thinking goes, if you write with your left hand, the right half of your brain is stronger.

FAMOUS LEFTIES

LEONARDO DA VINCI

JULIA ROBERTS

CHARLIE CHAPLIN

177

BUSTED!

THE QUESTION OF WHETHER LEFTIES

—10 percent of the population—are more creative has been studied a lot. The results are inconclusive. That means it's difficult to say with any certainty that left-handed people are more creative than right-handed people. A lot of lefties, or southpaws as they're also called, are creative. So are a lot of right-handed people. And the foundation that the idea is built on, that the right half of the brain is the more creative side, is oversimplified. The hemispheres of the brain don't function completely independent of each other. They work together and share information via a connective structure called the corpus callosum. And multiple regions can play a role in a skill or function, so it can be difficult to single out the seat of a creative ability.

President Barack Obama
IS A LEFTY.

MYTH

A SWALLOWED WATERMELON SEED WILL GROW INTO A WATERMELON IN YOUR STOMACH.

ORIGIN

Very rarely, swallowed seeds, usually larger ones, can lodge in the lungs or stomach and cause problems. If one of those problems were the seed growing into a fruit or vegetable, then a watermelon growing in your gut would cause a really big problem!

BUSTED!

A WATERMELON SEED WILL NEVER SPROUT AND GROW FRUIT IN YOUR GUT.

Your stomach simply does not have what a plant needs to grow—namely, sunlight!

Watermelons are true to their name: **THEY'RE 92 PERCENT WATER!**

MYTH

AN UGLY FACE WILL FREEZE PERMANENTLY INTO POSITION IF YOU MAKE IT TOO MUCH, OR IF SOMEONE SLAPS YOU ON THE BACK.

ORIGIN

This warning has been around a while. In the 1986 movie *One Crazy Summer*, two mean little girls making faces at a dog are stuck with ugly mugs after getting slapped on the back. And in an episode of *SpongeBob SquarePants*, SpongeBob and Patrick are left with ugly faces after making them too much.

BUSTED!

THERE'S NO SCIENCE TO BACK UP THE IDEA THAT A BACK SLAP WILL FREEZE A FACE

—ugly or not—in place. Nor is there any evidence that repeatedly making a face will fix it into position. The myth was probably made up by someone who was tired of looking at silly faces.

Contestants contort their faces into the ugliest mug possible at the annual WORLD GURNING CHAMPIONSHIP, in Egremont, England. Tommy Mattinson has taken home the top prize a record-setting 15 times.

MYTH

YOU SHOULD STARVE A FEVER, FEED A COLD.

ORIGIN

People used to believe that someone with a cold should eat to generate body heat, while someone suffering from a fever should do just the opposite—refrain from food—to lower their body temperature.

BUSTED!

DOCTORS WOULD NEVER ADVISE SOMEONE—especially someone who is sick—to starve themselves. And there is no strong evidence that not feeding a fever and feeding a cold gets rid of the ailments any quicker. A good rule of thumb, doctors say: If you feel hungry, eat. If not, it's OK to be food free for a short while. But even more important, they agree: Get plenty of rest and drink lots of fluids.

A fever may not feel good, but it can help fight off infection. A body temperature INCREASE OF JUST A FEW DEGREES CAN KILL OFF THE MICROBES INSIDE YOU that are making you sick.

SPILLING SALT IS BAD LUCK.

ORIGIN

We may take salt for granted now, but it was one of the earliest things to be coveted by people. Indeed, salt was so precious it was used as payment in ancient civilizations, which could rise and fall because of the mineral. So to spill salt would have been seen as a serious waste or offense. Spilling the seasoning really became linked with bad luck, though, thanks to Leonardo da Vinci's painting "The Last Supper." It depicts a scene from the Bible in which Jesus announces to his disciples that one of them will betray him. It was Judas, who in the painting is spilling a vessel of salt.

OCTOBER

Sunday	Monday	Tuesday	Wednesday	Thursday	Friday	Saturday
1	2	3	4	5	6	7
8	9	10	11	12	13	14
15	16	17	18	19	20	21
22	23	24	25	26	27	28
29	30	31	1	2	3	4

191

BUSTED!

SPILLING SALT DOES NOT CAUSE BAD THINGS TO HAPPEN.

It's an example of a superstition, or a belief in something that is not rational; there is no evidence to support the idea. So don't worry if you tip over the shaker at dinner. But if you still insist on being superstitious, some people say that you can undo your bad luck by throwing a pinch of salt over your left shoulder, where it will hit the devil—who is waiting there to cause trouble—squarely in the eye. But wouldn't throwing salt on purpose be worse than accidentally knocking it over? It's probably best to just clean it up, not throw more of it around.

Salt is a major source of sodium, an element that the BODY LITERALLY CAN'T LIVE WITHOUT.

193

THE SAFEST PLACE IN A HOME DURING AN EARTHQUAKE IS BENEATH A DOORWAY.

ORIGIN
Photographs of earthquake-rocked homes with only their door frames left standing gave the impression that they're the strongest part of a building.

Think you felt an earthquake? The United States Geological Survey, which tracks quakes, wants to know. VISIT HTTP://EARTHQUAKE.USGS .GOV/EARTHQUAKES/MAP/ and search your region for a recent quake, then click on the "DYFI?" link (short for "Did You Feel It?") and answer a few questions.

BUSTED!

DOOR FRAMES ARE OFTEN THE STRONGEST PART OF A BUILDING

if the building is made of unreinforced adobe, or sun-baked earth and straw, like those homes in the photos. But most homes today aren't made from adobe. They're made from materials that are just as strong if not stronger than a door frame. And many homes are reinforced, or strengthened, by concrete and steel additions. So, in most cases, you shouldn't stand in a doorway to keep safe. Instead, experts say, stay indoors and remember to do three things: Drop, cover, and hold. That means stop what you're doing, crawl under a sturdy piece of furniture, and hold on to it. If you can't crawl under something to protect yourself, get down low next to an interior wall or corner and cover the back of your neck and head with your hands. Stay away from windows, exterior walls, fireplaces, and any heavy items that could collide with you.

A PENNY PLACED ON RAILROAD TRACKS CAN DERAIL A TRAIN.

ORIGIN

Flattened coins are kind of fun. Some people get them from vending machines. Others place a penny on railroad tracks, step back, and wait. Urban legend holds that this method has caused trains to career off the tracks as they roll over the coins.

THERE'S NO RECORD OF A COIN LEFT ON RAILROAD TRACKS EVER CAUSING A TRAIN CRASH.

The train simply weighs much, much more than any coin it might encounter; it rolls right over it. A penny weighs 0.08 ounces (2.3 g), while a railcar can weigh more than 100 tons (90,720 kg). One ton is equivalent to 32,000 ounces—remember a penny isn't even one ounce! Putting a coin on railroad tracks could harm you, however. Each year, hundreds of people in the United States are killed while trespassing on train tracks.

YOU CAN TRAVERSE ASIA BY TRAIN ABOARD THE TRANS-SIBERIAN EXPRESS, which travels from Moscow to Vladivostok, Russia. The trip covers 5,753 miles (9,259 km) in a little over six days.

INDEX

Illustrations are indicated by **boldface.**

INDEX

For Mom & Dad, my first teachers. —EK

PUBLISHED BY THE NATIONAL GEOGRAPHIC SOCIETY

John M. Fahey, *Chairman of the Board and Chief Executive Officer*

Declan Moore, *Executive Vice President; President, Publishing and Travel*

Melina Gerosa Bellows, *Publisher; Chief Creative Officer, Books, Kids, and Family*

PREPARED BY THE BOOK DIVISION

Hector Sierra, *Senior Vice President and General Manager*

Nancy Laties Feresten, *Senior Vice President, Kids Publishing and Media*

Jennifer Emmett, *Vice President, Editorial Director, Kids Books*

Eva Absher-Schantz, *Design Director, Kids Publishing and Media*

Jay Sumner, *Director of Photography, Kids Publishing*

R. Gary Colbert, *Production Director*

Jennifer A. Thornton, *Director of Managing Editorial*

STAFF FOR THIS BOOK

Becky Baines, *Project Editor*
Kathryn Robbins, *Art Director*
Lori Epstein, *Senior Photo Editor*
Ariane Szu-Tu, *Editorial Assistant*
Callie Broaddus, *Design Production Assistant*
Margaret Leist, *Photo Assistant*
Cathleen Carey and Moriah Petty, *Editorial Interns*
Grace Hill, *Associate Managing Editor*
Joan Gossett, *Production Editor*
Lewis R. Bassford, *Production Manager*
Susan Borke, *Legal and Business Affairs*

PRODUCTION SERVICES

Phillip L. Schlosser, *Senior Vice President*
Chris Brown, *Vice President, NG Book Manufacturing*
George Bounelis, *Senior Production Manager*
Nicole Elliott, *Director of Production*
Rachel Faulise, *Manager*
Robert L. Barr, *Manager*

The National Geographic Society is one of the world's largest nonprofit scientific and educational organizations. Founded in 1888 to "increase and diffuse geographic knowledge," the Society's mission is to inspire people to care about the planet. It reaches more than 400 million people worldwide each month through its official journal, *National Geographic,* and other magazines; National Geographic Channel; television documentaries; music; radio; films; books; DVDs; maps; exhibitions; live events; school publishing programs; interactive media; and merchandise. National Geographic has funded more than 10,000 scientific research, conservation, and exploration projects and supports an education program promoting geographic literacy.

For more information, please visit nationalgeographic.com, call 1-800-NGS LINE (647-5463), or write to the following address:
National Geographic Society
1145 17th Street N.W.
Washington, D.C. 20036-4688 U.S.A.

Visit us online at nationalgeographic.com/books

For librarians and teachers: ngchildrensbooks.org

More for kids from National Geographic:
kids.nationalgeographic.com

For information about special discounts for bulk purchases, please contact National Geographic Books Special Sales: ngspecsales@ngs.org

For rights or permissions inquiries, please contact National Geographic Books Subsidiary Rights: ngbookrights@ngs.org

Paperback ISBN: 978-1-4263-1478-0
Reinforced library binding ISBN: 978-1-4263-1479-7

Printed in Hong Kong
14/THK/1

ABOUT THE ART

"To make these crazy collages, I start with a line drawing and layer pieces of collage on top. Backgrounds can start as torn paper doodles and then become landscapes or interiors. It's amazing what you can make from a scrap of paper!"

—Tom Nick Cocotos

Check out the artist online!
www.cocotos.com